MW00427096

Enjoy The Little Things In Life

An inspirational coloring book for Girls

by Carla Seaton

Enjoy The Little Things In Life; Copyright © 2017 Carla Seaton

Drawings; Copyright © 2017 Carla Seaton
www.carlasfunkyart.com

All rights strictly reserved under all International Copyright Conventions. No part of this book, including illustrations, may be reproduced, scanned, or distributed in any form or by any means, electronic or mechanical, including photocopying, recording or by any other information storage and retrieval system, without permission of the artist. Please do not participate in or encourage piracy of copyrighted materials in violation of the artist's rights.

Graphic Design, Page Layout:
Tony Locke, Armchair ePublishing
Anacortes, WA 98221
www.armchair-epulishing.weebly.com

This book is dedicated to all the women that raised me and made me who I am today.
(and boy, did that take a village!)
Grandma Dee, Flo Scheib, Pam Shelton
And of course
In loving memory of
Sandy MacDiarmid
And my mom Sandi Willock.
Love and miss you so much!

HEY YOU! HOPE YOU LIKE
YOUR NEW COLORING BOOK!
FIND OUT MORE ABOUT ME
AND MY FUNKY ART AT:
WWW.CARLASFUNKYART.COM

JOIN IN ON SOME
CONVERSATION ON FACEBOOK
WWW.FACEBOOK.COM/
CARLASFUNKYART

OR CHECK OUT MY ABC
ADJECTIVE BOOK ON
AMAZON:
"ANIMALS IN THE ALPHABET"

COLOR TEST PAGE

Create Your OWN PAGE

Create Your OWN PAGE

Create Your OWN PAGE

46811965R00033

Made in the USA
San Bernardino, CA
15 March 2017